BOWIE LEGENDS ALPHABET

Words by Robin Feiner

A is for **A**shes to Ashes. Funk to funky, Major Tom returns from his Space Oddity strung out and broken in this spiky new wave track from 1980. Bowie called the song an epitaph for his '70s era with a message from the Action Man: 'I'm happy, hope you're happy too.'

B is for **B**lackstar.
The ominous opener and title track to Bowie's final album, Blackstar is a ten-minute long swansong to his life. Delivered in two parts, the song is first unsettled and haunting, then embracing fate. Two days after the album's release, Bowie would pass, becoming stardust.

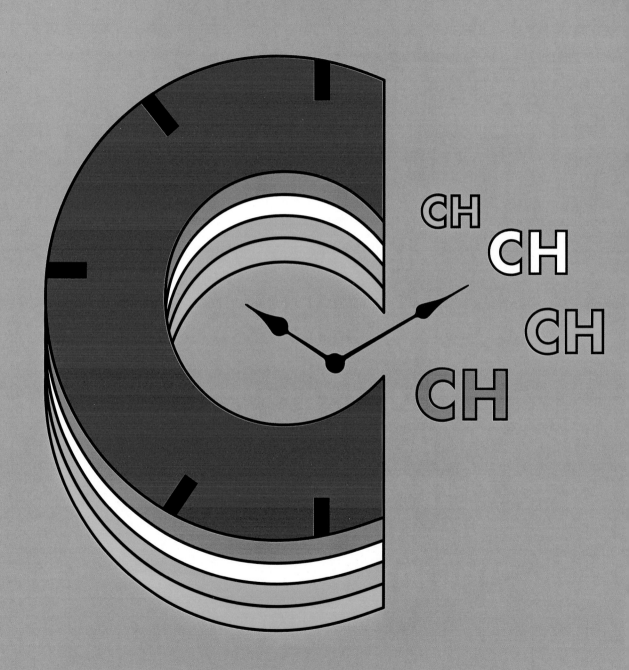

C is for **C**hanges.
Bursting with horns and piano, uplifting and defiant, 'Ch-Ch-Ch-Changes' is a call to arms for kids to turn and face the strange and be fearless and independent—just as the legend himself defied critics and their expectations. 'Time may change me, but I can't trace time!'

D is for Let's **D**ance. Classic '80s disco meets earnest, romantic lyrics in Let's Dance, where Bowie urges you to 'put on your red shoes and dance the blues.' Filmed in Australia, the legendary video stars two Indigenous lovers who, against all odds, 'sway under the moonlight, this serious moonlight.'

E is for **E**veryone Says 'Hi.' From 2002's Heathen album, this warm, breezy song about a holiday is actually about David's struggle to accept that his father's passing was forever, not just a couple of weeks. 'Said you sailed a big ship, said you sailed away. Didn't know the right thing to say.'

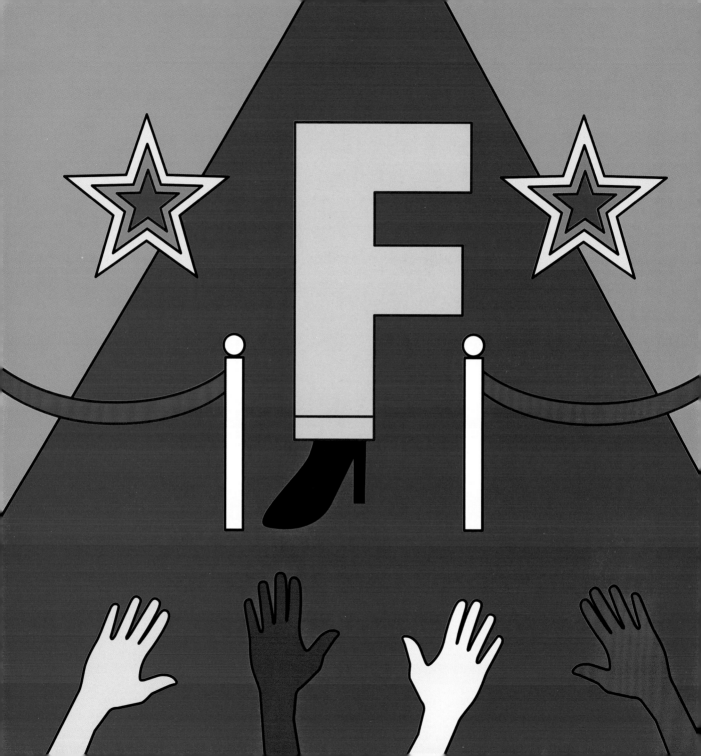

F is for Fame.
In 1974, Bowie's musical direction shifted from glam rock to disco, soul, and the jagged funk of Fame. Written with Beatles legend John Lennon, the song comments on the downside of celebrity. 'Fame! What you like is in the limo. Fame! What you get is no tomorrow!'

G is for **G**olden Years.
More funk followed Fame
with this groovy tune from
the Station to Station album.
Packed with swagger, hand-
claps, whistles, and doo-wops,
it's rumored to have been
written for Elvis Presley,
whom Bowie both adored
and shared a birthday with.
Two legends, one song!

Hh

H is for Heroes.
Recorded in Germany in 1977,
this uplifting anthem is one
of Bowie's greatest feats. Ten
years later, a live performance
of the song in Berlin would
inspire the crusade to reunite
East and West Germany and
demolish the Berlin Wall.
Such is the power of music!

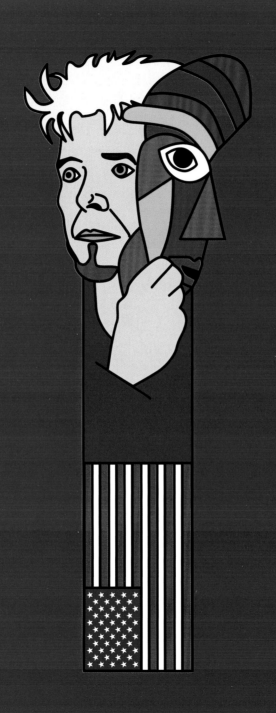

Ii

I is for I'm Afraid of Americans. By the '90s, Bowie was dabbling in gritty industrial rock and touring with genre legend Trent Reznor who calls Bowie a mentor. Sounding like machines fighting, I'm Afraid of Americans continues Bowie's career-long fear of and fascination with being an outsider in the USA.

J is for The **J**ean Genie. This legendary glam-rock stomp from the Aladdin Sane album has a simple, driving beat inspired by bluesman Bo Diddley. Full of attitude, it struts cool and carefree like a pair of well-worn jeans. Bowie called it a 'smorgas-bord of Americana' and his first real New York song.

K is for Kooks.
Appearing on the Hunky Dory album, Kooks was written for Bowie's baby boy, Duncan. 'Take a chance with a couple of kooks hung up on romancing?' Bowie asks, referring to himself and mum Angie. Duncan is now a Hollywood film director sharing David's love of sci-fi.

L is for Life on Mars?
This rousing pop song
with rich piano and soaring
strings is one of Bowie's
greatest. Combining his love
of space and escapism, the
song describes a lonely girl
walking 'through her sunken
dream . . . hooked on the silver
screen,' and asking, 'Is there
life on Mars?'

M is for Modern Love.
With its pulsing drums and
simple piano, Modern Love
is a joyful '80s hip-swinger.
From the album Let's Dance,
it combines an unabashed pop
sound with Bowie's skeptical
outlook on 'Modern Love!
Never gonna fall for . . .
Modern Love! Gets me
to the church on time!'

Nn

N is for New Killer Star.
This fuzzy rock track with
plenty of guitar swagger
is from 2003's Reality album.
A play on the words 'nuclear
star,' New Killer Star is Bowie
reacting to the burgeoning
Gulf War and offering a
way out: 'I got a better
way, ready, set, go.'

Oo

O is for Space **O**ddity. This psychedelic folk tune launched Bowie's love for space and his recurring character, astronaut Major Tom. It was released just in time for man's first steps on the moon. 'Ground Control to Major Tom, take your protein pills and put your helmet on!'

Pp

P is for Panic in Detroit.
Stuttering guitar, thundering
drums, and wailing vocals
pack Panic in Detroit with
energy and urgency. Singing
about the 1967 Detroit race
riots, Bowie based his lyrics
on stories told by his friend,
Detroiter Iggy Pop.

Q is for **Q**uicksand.
A dreamy folk tune from
the album Hunky Dory,
Quicksand features surreal
lyrics that contemplate the
meaning of life, spanning
topics that include Superman,
religion, and magic. 'I'm not
a prophet or a stone-age
man, just a mortal with the
potential of a superman.'

Rr

R is for **R**ebel Rebel. 'You've got your mother all in a whirl, she's not sure if you're a boy or a girl!' This punky dancefloor filler has become a timeless anthem for gender, self-expression, and partying. 'So hey babe, your hair's alright. Hey babe, let's go out tonight!'

S is for **S**tarman.
This legendary track is
the story of starman Ziggy
Stardust, who sends a message
of hope and resilience over
the radio to the kids listening
on Earth. 'He told us not to
blow it, 'cause he knows it's
all worthwhile!' So 'let all
the children boogie!'

T is for **T**ime.
Jaunty, cabaret-style piano opens this cheeky song from Aladdin Sane, pumped with musical theater melodrama. If life is a play, then Time is the bad guy coming for us all. 'He's waiting in the wings— he speaks of senseless things. His script is you and me, boy!'

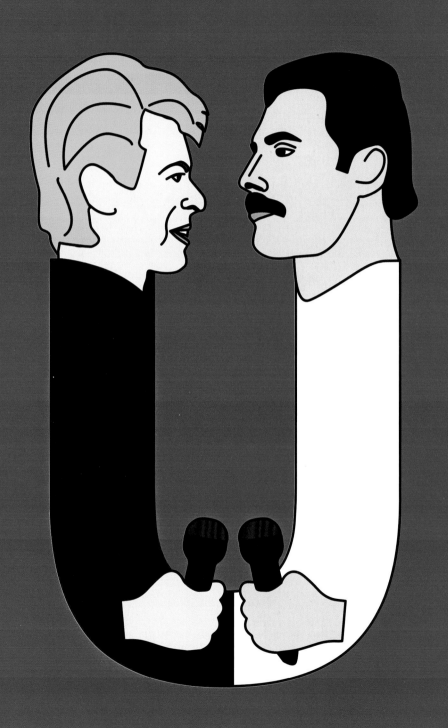

U is for **U**nder Pressure. This soaring duet with Queen features singers Freddie Mercury and David Bowie battling over their beliefs about love—cynical Bowie, 'slashed and torn,' versus Mercury, who pleads, 'Why can't we give love that one more chance?' 'This is our last dance,' the song proclaims, 'this is ourselves, under pressure!'

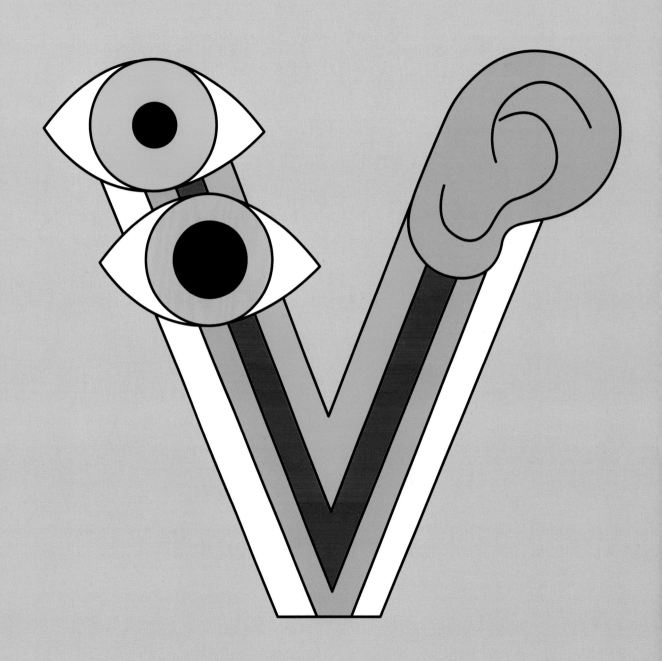

V is for Sound and Vision. Based on a cute, looped guitar lick, this track from the album Low builds playfully. It coincides with Bowie's stripped-back approach to life, seeking healthier inspirations for his songwriting. 'I will sit right down, waiting for the gift of sound and vision.'

W is for The Man Who Sold the World. With its mesmerizing guitar and trippy vocal effects, The Man Who Sold the World was a haunting folk song from 1970. But after Nirvana covered it for their MTV Unplugged performance, Bowie's music was introduced to a new generation—the '90s grunge kids.

The Next Day

X is for The Next Day.
A boisterous rock song, gruff and gloomy, The Next Day is Bowie at age 66 approaching his golden years while still raw with rock 'n roll. Singing 'They can't get enough of that doomsday song,' he signals he won't be going quietly into the night.

Y is for **Y**oung Americans. This big, soulful song is packed with contrasts. While Bowie's lyrics poke holes in the American dream of Barbie dolls and Ford Mustangs, the uplifting sax, gospel choir, and catchy chorus still charm us into a singalong. 'Aaaall night, she wants a Young American!'

Z is for **Z**iggy Stardust. This glam rock banger charts the fall from grace of Bowie's most legendary persona. After Ziggy Stardust saves the kids of Earth, it all goes to his head and blows up his ego. 'But, boy, could he play guitar,' he and 'the Spiders from Mars.'

The ever-expanding legendary library

EXPLORE THESE LEGENDARY ALPHABETS & MORE AT WWW.ALPHABETLEGENDS.COM

BOWIE LEGENDS ALPHABET
www.alphabetlegends.com

Published by Alphabet Legends Pty Ltd in 2022
Created by Beck Feiner
Copyright © Alphabet Legends Pty Ltd 2022

Printed and bound in China.

9780645487008